TIME MANAGEMENT SKILLS

LEARN THE SECRET OF GOOD TIME MANAGEMENT SKILLS

BY

THOMAS ERIKSSON

Disclaimer

TABLE OF CONTENTS

INTRODUCTION

There are so many people that state that there is not enough time in the day, when in fact there is. It all boils down to doing it like the big dogs. There are demands put on you everyday and it can be hard to manage or to perform each and every task in a timely manner and ensure their completion; however, in this book you will learn six main quality skills that are utilized in business and in everyday life that are practiced by some of the most successful people.

From evaluating yourself, all the way to understanding how to prioritize, this book will ensure that you are operating at your best. You will soon view yourself as a superhero as you truck along on that "To Do" list you seem to never complete. Welcome to a new and more productive life using great time management.

What is time management? To put it quite simply, time management is the management of your time. Sounds simple, right? Wrong! Time management is deemed a skill for a reason. Skills need to be practiced in order to build towards perfection. As you learn new time management skills you will be gaining control over your own life. A key to properly managing yourself is to know who and where you are going. This ultimately means you must know your own goals in life, which is covered in Chapter 1: Evaluate Yourself. In order to begin with your new path and leash on life, you will need to firstly know where you are headed. Good luck!

« CHAPTER 1 »

EVALUATE YOURSELF

Just as stated in the Introduction, you will need to know who you are and where you would like to go in life in order to evaluate yourself correctly. Those on top consistently evaluate themselves in different ways to ensure that they are working at their most optimal productivity level. They have already set their goals and when it seems there is a "bump in the road," they reevaluate to ensure that they are on the right path. In this chapter you are going to learn how to do this.

Before you begin going through this book you should know that there will be some exercises that you will need to do. You will need a small notebook that you can carry with you or something to that effect. A wonderful way to begin taking the reins on your life is to provide yourself with some great reasons why you want to manage your time better.

The first step to evaluate yourself is to think about why it is important to you to take control of your time. Is it better business? Is it to make more money? How about to spend more time at home? You can accomplish anything that you set out to if you understand the reasons on why you are taking this step. Write down the top four reasons why time management is crucial in your life.

Assess Behaviors

Now that you better understand yourself on why it is so important to you, you will now assess your time management behaviors to take a much clearer look at your daily schedule and behaviors. It will help you shine light on where your time may be going and how to fix it. In order to do this, you will read the behaviors that are listed. Assess how well it actually describes you.

There are four columns; the behavior, how often you do it, and then how important it is to you. The forth column is the rating. In order to find the rating you will take your answers from column 2 and 3, then multiply them. After you have gotten your ratings, circle the ones that are lower than 5. The ones that are circled are the items that you should work on.

Behavior	Often? Seldom = 1 Sometimes = 2 Frequently = 3	Important? Not At All = 1 Somewhat = 2 Very = 3	Rating
Have 3-4 personal and career goals that you are trying to reach.			
You use "to do" lists.			
You use a daily planner or			

calendar for events and tasks.			
Rank things by priority.			
Delegates responsibilities where you can.			
You have enough time to be with your family and friends.			
You are aware of your energy levels daily.			
You work on the most important tasks first.			
Instead of procrastinating on unpleasant tasks, you get it done by breaking it into pieces.			
You plan ahead and set aside time to complete big tasks.			
Schedule time for the interruptions in your day.			
You take care of yourself by giving yourself rewards for completing objectives.			
At the end of the day, you			

see that you have completed most of the "to do" list.			
You reward yourself at least twice a week.			
You set limits by saying no to things that others expect you to do for them.			
When you have to wait at a stop sign or light, you take a few deep breaths to relax.			
Schedule the amount of time daily that you devote to phone calls or emails.			
You strive to handle everything in your mail at one time.			
You are able to find an important paper or bill in less than 5 minutes.			
Each household member has his or her own list of responsibilities.			
You ask for help when you need it.			

Now that you have filled out your behavior ratings, take a look at the list. You will be able to discover what key tools you are not using. You will now need to ask yourself these questions to help deliver you to your new way of time management.

Am I doing all of the behaviors that I value?

What am I doing correctly for time management?

What are the practices that work the best for me?

What practices do I deem more important, and yet do not do often?

What are the reasons for my actions?

What are 2-3 new behaviors that would give me more control over my life?

Setting Your Goals

This is another part of evaluating yourself. Without the knowledge of where you want to go in life, you will not be able to schedule your time so that is benefits you. You life is made up of very small to big choices that you will need to make.

Those who are "making it big" use this method of goal setting, even if they are unaware of it. The method is called SMART. SMART stands for:

S – Specific

M – Measurable

A – Attainable

R – Rewarding

T – Timely

If you neglect just one of these guidelines, then you will probably mess up your goals. The key force that makes you drive towards a goal or holds you back is you.

Specific

If you keep your goals specific then you will be able to see your goal clearly. This mean you will be able to achieve it. When you are making your list of goals, ensure that they are specific and you write them down. This is critical. When you are working on making sure that your goal is specific, you will program your mind to work for you.

Measurable

Ensure that the goal that you set is measurable in terms of progress. This is important so that you are aware when you hit a goal. Believe it or not, there are some people who have their goals in their minds with no measure of progress. Once they have hit the goal they are unaware of it and then do not realize when they hit it. Thus, they waste time on completing a task that they have already achieved.

Attainable

An attainable goal is one that you are able to reach using a realistic path. This does not mean you need to set your goals low, but you need to ensure that the goal is realistic. For example, a writer is not going to be able to write three novels and tour the Untied States in a single month. This is not an attainable goal.

Rewarding

A goal that is completed is a goal that is rewarding. Imagine how you will feel once you have completed that goal. You can even offer yourself a reward once you have completed the goal. It is suggested to reward yourself two times a week for a couple of the goals that you have completed.

Timely

The fifth key to the goal setting guidelines is to ensure that your goal is completed in a timely manner. However, in order to do it in a timely manner, you will need to understand how much time you will need for the task. You will need to make sure that you set a deadline for the goals and follow them. It will ensure that you stop the procrastination.

Setting Short and Long term Goals

When you are setting goals it is important to have effective time management skills. Your goals will become more powerful once you put them on paper or in writing. The more 'SMART' your goals are, the better chance you have of achieving them. Decisions are simpler to make when you know exactly what you want.

You will need to choose only a few goals to start with. There are so many people that try to achieve many goals at one time and then they often times fail due to not using the SMART method. Here are some tips in order to help you ensure that you keep manageable goals, as well as achieve them.

In order to accomplish the goals, you will need to perform a series of tasks. Begin with the word "to" and then include a verb of action. For example, "to build", "to climb", or "to finish".

Give specific details when you add your action. "To complete a nail and hair design course."

Note how you will be able to measure the success along the way. "To walk 4 times around the track, 3 times a week." Notice how there are ways to measure the success of the goal.

Ensure that your goal is realistic and that it does not depend on unforeseen factors that are not in your control. Revise it if you deem it necessary.

State the end of the goal. Write down the outcome that you want to happen from the goal. "So that I can have extra stamina for the marathon."

Goal Exercise

In order to get a clear manageable goal set into place, you will need to sit down and figure a few things out. Ask yourself these questions:

What would you like to change about how you manage your time?

What are the top three goals that you want to set for your lifetime? For example, do you want to make $85,000 a year? That would be a lifetime goal.

You will need to list 3-4 goals that you would like to accomplish in the next five years. Have you heard of the five-year plan? This is it.

This may not seem pleasant at first thought, but it will definitely light a fire under you. Pretend that you only have six months to live. What do you want to ensure that you do in those six months? Then you will need to put them in order of priority.

How can you break those goals up into manageable pieces? This is where you make smaller goals out of your large ones to ensure that you complete the larger goal. Celebrate your success and reward yourself on your way to the bigger picture.

« Chapter 2 »
Prepare In Advance

In order to obtain success, you will need to prepare for your advancement through your goals. Without being prepared, it can cause you to stumble. You will need to ensure how to take advantage of your prime time (covered in Chapter 3). Here are ways that you can ensure that you are prepared, from planning ahead to learning how to tell people that you are not doing their tasks for them.

Time Management Steps

Plan ahead for the times where you have more energy. Plan your important tasks during this time.

Save the routine work for the lower energy parts of your day.

Find a way to stretch the periods of great energy.

Strive to ensure that your interruptions are at a minimum.

Use some energizers to give you boosts of energy when you need it. Those who normally need a boost are those who take care of others like young ones, teachers, senior caretakers, and more. Although energy drinks are not suggested, a dose of vitamin B complex should do the job.

Take a few breaks to perform relaxation exercises. This will keep your mind clear and ready to accomplish your goals.

Ensure that you are eating healthy to ensure that you are functioning at your optimal performance levels physically, as well as mentally. Those that eat a diet high in bad fats are also sluggish and make poor decisions.

Take action early on, in order to cut out stress or tension that you may be feeling as a result of meeting the needs of others.

Plan your day in order to take full advantage of your time.

Take Responsibility

There are many people who automatically blame lack of time on others. "It isn't my fault that I was late, my kid wouldn't hurry up." Blaming others for your lack of time will never help you. Accept the responsibility for you being late and how you spend your time. You will gain more power over your life. When you take a look back and connect the choices to the outcomes you will see a clearer picture of how you can ensure that you save time. You are your own responsibility.

Learn to Say No

You need to learn how to say no. It is one thing to blame others for wasting your time; however, it is another to allow them to actually do so. You will need to develop the skill of saying no. This ability will enable you to have better control over your life. Here are ways to handle it.

Be very clear about what it is that you want and what you do not want. Be clear about communicating it to others.

Evaluate the requests you receive. Do you have the time for a task given by someone else? Will this task get you closer to one of your own goals? Do you actually want it?

Tactfully reject or accept it as soon as you can. Avoid giving answers like "We will see," or "I will get back to you". These will force you to deal with them later when you are absolutely busy. Either you can fit it in the schedule or you cannot.

Trade the feelings of guilt with the feeling of satisfaction. You will not be overcommitted, and then you will be able to get things done.

« CHAPTER 3 »
SCHEDULE YOUR TIME

Another important time management skill that you will need to use, just like the top dogs. It is how to schedule your time more efficiently. In this chapter you will learn everything there is to know about this specific time management tool. Break out that handy notebook that you have been using to evaluate yourself and your life.

Finding Your Prime Time

Before you can begin scheduling your time effectively you will need to understand your *prime time*. Everyone has a different timetable that is different. Have you heard of "morning people" or "night people"? Well, this is a direct reference to their prime times. One key aspect of effective time management is to figure out your own prime time. The prime time is when you have the most energy. This will help you discover when to schedule the tasks that need your ultimate attention.

In order to do this you will pick a typical day in order to graph your personal energy level. You will need to be prepared to spend about 2-3 minutes every hour during that day in order to record your energy levels on the chart example below.

At the top of each hour you will put a dot on the box where it best represents your energy level. At the end of the day you will connect your dots. Examine the peaks and the valleys of your energy. Make note of where you have the most energy.

TIME	Very High	High	Medium	Low	Sleep
5 AM					
6 AM					
7 AM					
8 AM					
9 AM					
10 AM					
11 AM					
12 PM					
1 PM					
2 PM					
3 PM					
4 PM					
5 PM					
6 PM					
7 PM					
8 PM					

9 PM					
10 PM					
11 PM					
12 AM					

After you have dotted and connected, look at the peak in the energy level. This is where you will want to schedule the most important or the most demanding tasks that you need to complete throughout the day.

Importance of Scheduling

The importance of scheduling is typically only known when it is not followed out correctly. It is because when the schedule is not effectively done, then it means that the person will feel the effects by not getting tasks done in a timely manner. Scheduling will help you accomplish goals and complete tasks. Once you do this properly, scheduling will help you:

Understand what you are able to accomplish realistically.

Ensure that you have enough time for important tasks.

Add contingency time for interruptions.

You will avoid taking on too much during your days.

You will work steady toward goals.

Have enough time for friends and family, hobbies, and exercising.

Achieve great balance between work and home.

Schedule for Scheduling

It may sound odd, but you will need to set time aside everyday in order to schedule effectively. So, in essence you will schedule time in order to schedule. If you do not do this, then you will not have a proper schedule. This is where that little notebook will come in handy if you are not a very busy person; however, it is best to utilize a planner for your scheduling. You can pick one up from the local retail store where office supplies are offered. If you do not want to do this, you can print blank calendar templates to make use of. Here are the steps to do so.

Step 1: Identify Your Available Time

You will begin by establishing the time that you would like to make available for work. Block this out by drawing a line at the start and at the end of this time block. Ensure that you do not schedule anything in between those time blocks. If you have a work schedule that you are given weekly, then you will need to block the time out for transporting to work and then starting, as well as the end of your work days on the appropriate dates.

Step 2: Schedule the Important Tasks

Make sure that you allow time for interruptions. If you have kids, then this will be extremely important to do. You know that you do not have peace all hours of the day. For example, when you have a young child you will need to schedule almost double the amount of time for one task than you would normally need. The same goes for overseeing a team of workers.

Step 3: Schedule the High Priority Tasks

Make a "to do" list and figure out what tasks have the higher priority. Schedule those as urgent tasks. Try to arrange the tasks using your prime time, as well as when the deadline is for the tasks.

Step 4: Schedule Contingency Moments

Next, you will need to ensure that you schedule time to cope with emergencies or contingencies. Experience will be able to tell you how much time you will need to schedule per task. Typically, the more unpredictable your life or job is; the more you will need to schedule. Frequent interruptions will eat into your schedule and throw everything off.

Step 5: Schedule Flexible Time

The time that you have left after scheduling your time is your flexible time. It is available for you to hit your personal goals. For example, maybe you are training for a marathon and you have some flexible time. Maybe it would be a good idea to take that one hour extra that you have open and dedicate it to training.

Step 6: Analyze the Tasks

If you have reached step five and you do not have much flexible time, then you will need to go back through the steps 2-4 and ask the question of where you can redo your schedule in order to achieve a better balance.

One of the most important ways that you are able to build a successful schedule where you have some flexible time is to delegate tasks. Whether you are overseeing a team or scheduling a household, you can delegate tasks to another person that they can handle. It will free up a bit of your time and offer you a better-balanced schedule.

Key Points of Scheduling

Scheduling is the practice of planning how you will use your time on a daily basis. Doing it will offer you the maximum effectiveness of your day, as well as lower your stress levels.

Identify the time that is available.

Block out the time for important tasks.

Schedule high priority tasks and vital home tasks.

Block out contingency times.

Schedule your tasks that need to be addressed for your personal goals.

Analyze the tasks to identify those that can be delegated to someone else.

Learn How to Ask for Help and Delegate

If you think delegating tasks is difficult you need to evaluate the reasons why. Read over this list and see if there is any that apply to you.

You can complete the task better than someone else that you would ask for help.

You are too busy to delegate the tasks.

You feel guilty for putting your work on someone else.

You do not believe that you can depend on someone to help you.

You do not like to ask for help.

You are afraid that you may become dispensable.

You do not want to be viewed as weak or in need of any help.

You do not want to be viewed as if you cannot handle your responsibilities.

When you get a new task or request, evaluate the task by answering these questions:

How important is it?

Is the request a reasonable one and is the result achievable?

Do you need help to accomplish the task?

Does the project require your personal attention, or is someone else able to do the job?

Who is the best person to carry out the job?

Is the best person to do the job available within that timeframe?

In order to improve the delegating skills and to make others want to work for you:

Choose the right person for the task.

Ensure that you communicate clearly for the best results.

Give a simple and concise set of instructions.

Allow the questions to be asked anytime.

Give the task a good and reasonable deadline.

Treat the person that you delegate tasks to as your partner.

Give your assistant some responsibilities for reporting any progress to you about the tasks.

Ensure that you show appreciation to those that you delegate tasks too.

Share the credit for the success of the tasks or projects.

Decision Making Techniques and Skills

People use decision-making skills in order to solve problems by selecting one option from a list of options. However, decision-making can be difficult. Those with good decision-making skills utilize good decision-making techniques. Here is a guide in order to make an informed decision.

Identify the purpose of the decision. What is the problem that needs to be solved? Why should it be solved?

Gather up information. What factors are involved in the problem?

Identify any principles to get a sense of any alternatives. What are the standards and the criteria of judgment that needs to be met by the solution?

Brainstorm and list any possible choices. Generate different ideas for possible outcomes or solutions.

Evaluate every choice in the terms of the consequences. Use the standards and the judgment criteria in order to determine the pros and cons of every alternative.

Determine the best solution. This is much easier when you have already gone through the steps above.

Put your decision into action. Transform your decision into actions by making a plan of action. Then you will execute your plan.

Evaluate the outcome of the decision and the steps of action. What are the lessons that you can learn from the decision?

Writing an Effective Action Plan

This will help you with the decision making process. Here are the steps in order to make sure that you are executing the plans that you have laid in front of you.

Clarify every goal. You can use a visual aid to get you motivated or excited. For example, if you make the goal of publishing your manuscript, then make a collection of pictures to have a visual aid of what you want. This will help your excitement when plotting your schedule for your goals.

Write out a list of different actions that you will need to do in order to follow through with your goal or decision. Do not judge what you write on the paper. You will go through the action list to decide what actions are relevant and what actions will help you.

Organize the list into a plan of action. Decide on whether the order will help you with your goal. Rearrange the actions and the ideas in order to produce a realistic plan of action.

Monitor the execution of the plan and regularly review the plan on a regular basis. It will make sure that your plan of action is followed through and your goal is met. You should use your planner for these plans.

« Chapter 4 »
Start Your Day Early

The thought of getting out of bed early may make you cringe. However, those who get out of that comfortable sleeping zone proves to accomplish more every day, and in their lives in general. Getting up early will allocate you more time in one day to achieve your goals and get those pesky "to do" lists done. It will open up more time to hit your personal goals and you will not stress about not having enough time.

The morning sets the tone for the day and the tone will have a direct effect on how your day will be spent. You can either be sluggish and disorganized, or you can use these tips to attack your day and rule your life. Here are the tips to help you take hold of the day, even when you do not want to get out of bed.

Tip #1: Hit snooze.

Your mind may be blown because of this first tip. You may be asking yourself why you should hit the snooze button when the point is to actually get of bed and to get going. Well, it is quite simple. You can hit the snooze button one time, and only one time. It will allow you to have that extra 10 minutes where you will be able to get out of the sleep fog. It offers you better control over your thoughts once your feet hit the floor.

Tip #2: Brighten up your area

Research shows that waking up to brighter colors will increase the person's mental agility, as well as increase their confidence and make them happier overall. This means paint those dark walls, get a brighter comforter, and make sure that the curtains match your new brighter comforter. Greens and yellows are the best colors to use when you decorate your bedroom.

Tip #3: Remember to smile

When you look in the mirror for the first time every morning, smile. It will reduce your stress first thing in the morning. It will release the feel-good endorphins inside your body. Then, keep smiling through the day even if you have to fake it.

Tip #4: Turn the volume up

When you are getting ready in the mornings put on your own concert with your favorite bands. Make sure the music is uplifting and energetic. Research shows that music will make you feel happier and will improve the blood vessel functions, as well as reduce your stress.

Tip #5: Eat a good breakfast.

Breakfast is the most important meal of the day. Why? It is because your body will use the nourishment that is offered in the early hours to get you going and help keep you going most of the day. Refuel at lunch to keep that energy going.

Ensure that your meals are healthy or it will have an adverse effect.

Tip #6: Catch up on events.

Take a little bit of time to catch up on events in relationship to you and your work. Staying in the "know" will ensure that you are prepared for the bumps in the road. It will ensure that you are prepared and can handle events that may happen.

Tip #7: Prioritize your tasks.

We all have "to do" lists, and by now you already understand the importance of having one of these lists on a daily basis. Scan your planner or calendar to get a clear picture of what you are supposed to do that day. Complete the most important tasks first. Doing this before you begin your day will allow you to have an easier day. It will prevent you from scrambling through to ensure that you get at least half of your list done.

Tip #8: Schedule time for yourself

Whether you need to work on a personal goal or you need to relax, make sure that you schedule time for yourself. Waking up early will allow you to schedule a little time before you begin your day working for and taking care of other people.

Tip #9: Get to work early.

You will take some stress away by avoiding the typical commute to work by leaving the house a bit earlier. Therefore, if there is an accident or heavy traffic, you will not stress about being late. You will arrive early or at least on time without trying to catch up.

« CHAPTER 5 »
ORGANIZATIONAL SKILLS

Organizing your life is extremely important in your personal and your professional life. In this chapter, you are going to learn how to organize all aspects of your life in order to make sure that you are operating to your fullest potential. From your bedroom to your office, you will learn how to organize your life. You will need to take hold of your life by spending some time to clean out the clutter.

De- Clutter Your Life

Many time management specialists agree that in order to be effective with time management, you will also need to learn how to organize, as well as de-clutter the spaces where you live and where you work. Research shows that time is wasted every day by searching for items that end up getting lost in the shuffle. You will need to begin by de-cluttering your living space and branching out. Here is a quick overview on how to organize your organizations of the home.

Make a plan. Write a list of every part of your home or the office in which you should de-clutter.

Pick your target. Begin with an area that will make the biggest impact on the space.

Decide on a date. Set aside a certain day and a certain time that you will tackle the area. Mark it on your planner and make sure that you follow through with it. It will only take a few minutes to clean out a drawer so make sure that you do not fall in to the trap of thinking you should block out large blocks of time for a small task.

Get some support. If you are having issues staying on track, share the goal with a friend. Have someone check in with you on the progress and someone to celebrate with once it is a success. It will help to motivate you.

Ideas to Organize Rooms in Your Home

Here are ideas on how you can organize your home to better find a permanent place for items that get lost in the shuffle. Keep in mind that creativity is key when organizing your home. Just because one item is meant for a purpose does not mean it can not be used for another. Take these tips and apply them to cut down on time that you could use to hit your goals.

Kitchen

Use an expandable rail like a curtain rod underneath your sink to hang the cleaning bottles on. Put small baskets under the bottles to hold the scrub brushes or rags.

Use a decorative magnetic rack to store your knives against the wall near your cooking area.

Use some tension rods as dividers for the cabinets. They will allow you to store cutting boards and trays on their side, thus offering more space and quicker finds.

Use a magazine holder to store your aluminum foil, wax paper rolls, and plastic wrap in your cabinet.

Use a hanging magazine rack to put your pot lids on. It can be fastened to the cabinet door on the inside.

Hang the pots and pans from your ceiling using a pot rack and hooks.

Attach magnetic pieces to small canisters for spices. Put these spices on the side of your refrigerator.

Add wire racks to your refrigerator to offer more shelf space and storage.

Keep the bulk items like sugar and flour in stackable bins and drawers.

Attack some under shelves in the cabinet to make more shelf space.

Closets

Use pants hangers to hang up boots in the closet.

Use some crown molding for heel wracks on the wall.

Label the hangers for specific clothing.

Turn all of the hangers in your closet backwards. Once you wear an article of clothing put the hanger back the right way. After one month go to your closet and rid your space of those clothes that you do not wear.

Use some dividers on the closet shelf to store sweaters.

Use a sliding rack for belts and ties.

Use a hanger to hang eyewear on and store them in your closet instead of a drawer.

Use shower curtain hooks for hanging your purses or other bags.

Use some command hooks on the back of your closet door for jewelry.

If you have a lot off boots, cut some pool noodles to place in the boots inside the closet so they do not fall over and take up the closet floor.

Store sheet sets inside the pillowcases inside the bedroom where they belong.

Bathroom

Attach your tweezers on the inside of your medicine cabinet using a magnet.

Use some magnetic strips on the back of the medicine cabinet door to store bobby pins, scissors, and other small metal pieces.

Use PVC pipes in order to store your hair appliances behind the cabinet door.

Screw a magazine rack to the inside of the cabinet door to store the hair appliances in.

Make a storage spot using mason jars for items like Q-tips, make up sponges, cotton balls, and other items.

Make a pretty bracelet and rubber band holder by using a glass bottle on a shelf. Drop them over the bottles to hold them.

You can use a paper towel holder for rubber bands and bracelets.

Put all of the makeup in one spot.

Put a shelf over the bathroom door for things you do not need too often.

Hang some baskets on the rails in order to store towels and different shower supplies.

Laundry Room

Use a shoe organizer for the cleaning supplies.

Put your washer and your dryer on a shelf in order to offer room for a few laundry baskets to store items.

Hang a small ladder from the ceiling in order to add spots for air drying clothing that cannot be dried.

Garage

Use bungee cords as ball storage.

Use pegboard with movable hoods to organize sports gear.

Separate screws, nails, batteries, and other small items in jars by making a shelf and screwing the lids to the shelf. You can then have removable hanging storage jars.

Invest in plastic storage bins for storage. Label them and stack them out of the way.

Crafting Area

Use decorated coffee cans on the wall for yarn storage shelving.

Use a pegboard to place hooks and cups for storing small items in an accessible spot that is out of the way.

Use plastic drawers for storage and label them.

Hang appliances like glue guns on the pegboard using hooks. Keep a small trashcan under the crafting table to ensure there is no trash build up.

Instead of a typical chair, use a stool with a compartment for storage.

Media

You can use an ottoman for storage for DVDs and CDs.

Use decorative boxes to store the DVD cases in.

Use a CD binder and get rid of the jewel boxes.

Label cords using decorative or colored tape and a permanent marker.

Use a bench or a window seat for the storage of vinyl records.

General Tips

Use jars with chalkboard paint to label the jars.

Use labels on baskets to store frozen bags in the freezer.

Cut shoe organizers and put them on the inside of cabinet doors for extra storage spaces.

Use candy tins that are labeled for small items like paper clips, staples, and other office supplies.

Repurpose different containers like paint cans for crayons and more.

Use some small containers for a "to do" list kit on your refrigerator. Add a magnet on the cans with a notepad.

Office

Purge the office of anything that is trash or unneeded.

Gather up all like items and put them in one spot out of the way.

Establish the work zones. You will need to keep the items for certain work in that specified working area.

Label everything. If you are using boxes or containers, ensure that you label the container to ensure that you do not go hunting for items and to ensure that you put things away where they belong.

Revise the filing system. Instead of using paper filing storage, use a scanner to upload images of the documents to a flash drive or another digital storage device. For the items that you need to keep the hard copy of, use a storage box out of the way.

Create a folder for meetings. Put all of the items that need to be discussed in one folder in one specific spot.

Clear off your desk. Remove everything that does not have a spot on the desk. Use some desktop organizers or even containers in order to organize different items on the desk. Use some trays for papers and small containers for other small items.

Organize the drawers. Put the items that are used together in one drawer. For example, store all mailing supplies in one drawer.

Separate the inboxes. If you work with regular people then create a folder, inbox, or tray for each person.

Clear the piles. Sort through piles of items and papers to ensure that you do not have miscellaneous items and papers sitting around.

Sort your mail over a trashcan so you can throw out the trash as you go through it.

Assign dates for discard. You do not need to keep all papers. Assign dates to when the paper can be thrown away or shredded. Some legal or financial documents will need to be kept for a certain period of time. Ensure that you know what those dates are for each piece.

Use storage boxes. The boxes are inexpensive and will keep the files together and out of your way.

Use magazine boxes or even binders to store the magazines or catalogs that you want to keep. Make sure that you actually do need them for reference and not to just keep them for a "just in case" type of situation.

Make a reading folder. Designate a file for articles to read later.

Straighten the desk at the end of the day so you can begin work right away. It will only take a couple minutes versus all the time you waste looking for items or cleaning it later all at once.

Stack mason jars on their side for pen, pencil, and marker storage. You can even use it for paper clips and so much more.

Use a frame to hang a piece of fitted pegboard for your supplies in a nice looking manner.

Use a small old shutter to attach to the wall for a mail holder.

Attach three magazine holders to the bottom of a shelf. It will allow you to store important items like outgoing mail and more.

Use wall brackets for bookends or ways to house magazines and folders.

Use makeup organizers as drawer dividers for your office supplies.

Use an old window for a memory board. Use chalkboard paint and tack board on the windows to transform it for a message board. Hang it on the wall.

Convert a storage chest into a workstation by using file cabinet racks for files and put tack board on the lid.

« CHAPTER 6 »
INCREASE YOUR PRODUCTIVITY

In order to increase your productivity, you will need to throw out the bad habit of procrastination. In this chapter you are going to learn how to fix the habit of procrastination.

"Hard work is often the easy work you did not do at the proper time." ~ Bernard Meltzer

Have you spent the day scrambling to get things done only to see the most important tasks on your list to be left untouched? This happens when you procrastinate. This has also probably left you scrambling the next day, as well as putting you in a bad mood. What is it?

The definition of procrastination is the action of putting off tasks that you should be doing. This typically happens with everyone from time to time. The difference between typical people and those who make millions is the fact that they can recognize and correct procrastination before it has an effect on our goals. Procrastination will steal away many opportunities throughout your entire life; professionally and personally.

Causes of Procrastinating

There are typical reasons why people may procrastinate. Here are a few of the most known situations that may cause a person to procrastinate.

If you decide that you will wait for the proper mood.

If you decide to wait for the right time to complete the task.

If you take a look at the way you organize your work, then you may notice some other reasons why you procrastinate. Some other reasons that you may find will include:

Having a lack of clear goals

Underestimating the difficulty of a task

Underestimating the time that is required to complete a task

Having unclear standards for the outcome of a task

Having a feeling as if the task is imposed on you

The task is too ambiguous

Underdeveloped skills for decision-making

Having a fear of failure or even success

Being a perfectionist

Solution: Just do it

Tools for Time Management

Now that you are fully aware of how to effectively manage your time, you will need to learn about the tools that many well-known people use. Given here in this section is a list of tools, as well as a description and how to use them.

Planners: A planner will allow you to have a spot to jot down lists and schedule times and dates. They normally Offer a calendar, an agenda, and a contacts list all in one spot. To use this effectively, make sure that you check it every morning to plan your day. When you are given a new task you will need to schedule it right away.

Device Calendars: If you have a smart phone or a tablet then you are in luck. You have many time management apps at your fingertips. Utilize them and you will see a large increase in your productivity.

Here are some time management apps that you can take advantage of:

RescueTime: This is a tool that will run on your computer and will record how long you are spending on different applications or activities as you move through your list. It will also generate an analysis of how you are using your time.

ActiveWords: This is a smart program that will allow you to assign different abbreviations to lengthy information. For instance, you are able to customize it to your specifications.

MindMeister: This is a cloud-based tool that will allow you to customize a visual mind map. It is best for those who are visual people. They can see their goals rather than try to stick with lists.

List.ly: Just like MindMeister is for visual people, List.ly is for those who use lists.

Toggl: This is an easy program that is used for those who like to keep track of how long they are working on a certain project. You are able to try to beat the last recorded time to boost your productivity.

Grid Analysis: This is a tool that was designed in order to help you make decisions. It will allow you to list options in a table and then form it with columns.

StayFocused: This is a great program that will ensure that you do not waste time on those sites that you should not be on while you are working. There are people who waste time with other websites and end up using their time on tasks that do not get them anywhere.

Conclusion

Thank you again for purchasing this book!

We hope this book was able to help you in your needs and to satisfy your reading pleasures.

Finally, if you enjoyed this book, please take the time to share your thoughts and post a review on Amazon. It would be greatly appreciated!

Thank you and good luck!

Check Out Our Other Books

Please feel free to visit www.ecarepublishing.com to discover other books we have available.

We would be honored if you participated in our email notifications where you can get early bird announcements of our new upcoming books.